The Majesty of
NATCHEZ

BY STEVEN BROOKE

PELICAN PUBLISHING COMPANY

GRETNA 2001

For
Suzanne and Miles

Stanton Hall

Copyright © 1969 by Paddle Wheel Publications
Copyright © 1981, 1999 by Pelican Publishing Company
All rights reserved
First Pelican edition: Tenth printing, October 1986
Eleventh printing, October 1993
Second Pelican edition: First printing, February 1999
Thirteenth printing, September 2001
ISBN: 1-56554-158-8
LC: 98-48354
Printed in Hong Kong

Published by Pelican Publishing Company, Inc.
1000 Burmaster Street, Gretna, Louisiana 70053

ACKNOWLEDGMENTS

I extend my deepest gratitude to the following for their contributions to this book. Dr. Milburn Calhoun, president of Pelican Publishing Company, for his continued support of my work. Patrick Davis, my editor at Pelican, and the Pelican staff for all their assistance. Mr. William Garbo, landscape architect, for introducing me to the beauties of Natchez and for his invaluable assistance with the research and logistics. Ron and Mimi Miller, founders of the Historic Natchez Foundation, for their enthusiasm, dedication, and scholarship, and for generously granting me permission to borrow freely from their historically accurate *Great Houses of Natchez*. Mr. Roger Saterstrom and Ms. Patricia Rogers of Natchez Pilgrimage Tours. Mrs. Grace MacNeil of *Elms Court*, for her graciousness and hospitality. Mr. H. Hal Garner, for providing me with invaluable assistance and a base of operations in Natchez. Ms. Margaret Tillman, whose lovely smile on page 5 welcomes us to Natchez. Ms. Laura Cerwinske, my friend and colleague, for her advice and editing. My special thanks to the generous residents of Natchez, who are truly its majesty.

Mrs. Grace MacNeil, *Elms Court*
Elizabeth Boggess, *Cherry Grove*
Mr. and Mrs. Hyde D. Jenkins, *Hawthorne*
Natchez Garden Club, *House on Ellicott's Hill, Magnolia Hall*
Pilgrimage Garden Club, *Longwood, Stanton Hall, The Towers, King's Tavern*
Mrs. Alma Carpenter, *The Elms*
Mr. and Mrs. J. R. Whatley, *Cherokee*
Mr. and Mrs. Richard Campbell, *Edgewood*
Mr. and Mrs. Bazile Lanneau, *Fair Oaks*
Mr. and Mrs. James W. Overton, *Mistletoe*
Mr. and Mrs. Larry Brown, *Mount Repose*
Mississippi State Society of the DAR, *Rosalie*
Mr. and Mrs. Albert Metcalfe, *The Parsonage*
Mr. and Mrs. Jack Benson, *D'Evereux*
Mrs. George Morrison, *Green Leaves*
Mrs. Lawrence Adams, *Oakland*
Mrs. C. E. Ratcliffe, *Routhland*
Dr. Homer Wittington, *Twin Oaks*
Auburn Garden Club, *Auburn*
Robert C. Blackwell, Harry Gorst, *Gloucester*
Mrs. Hunter Goodrich, *Monteigne*
Mrs. Josephine Nall, *Richmond*
Mr. and Mrs. William Heins, *Dunleith*
Mr. and Mrs. George Guido, *Glenburnie*
Mrs. Mackenzie Nobles, *Lansdowne*
Mr. and Mrs. Ron Riches, *Monmouth*
Mrs. Catherine Morgan, *Ravenna*
Dr. and Mrs. George Moss, *Texada*
Mr. and Mrs. Roger Smith, *Coyle House*
Dr. and Mrs. William Calhoun, *Elgin*
Mrs. Jeanette Feltus, *Linden*

Newton Wildes, R. E. Cannon, *The Briars*
Dr. and Mrs. Richard Boyer, *Glen Auburn*
Robert Pulley and Rivet Hedderal, *Governor Holmes House*
Mrs. Ethel Banta, *Hope Farm*
Mr. and Mrs. W. S. Perkins, *Shields Town House*
Mr. and Mrs. Larry Christianson, *The Burn*
Mr. Gene Weber, *Weymouth Hall*
Mr. and Mrs. Jim Love, *Airlie, Wilkins Town House*
Dr. and Mrs. Robert Barnes, *Barnes House*
Mrs. Stanley Diefenthal, *Brandon Hall*
Mr. and Mrs. Don DuPriest, *Choctaw*
Mr. and Mrs. Tom McNeil, *Cottage Gardens*
Mr. and Mrs. S. Barnett Serio Jr., *Dixie*
Mr. and Mrs. John Tillman, *Peter Crist House*
Mr. John Rice Baker, *Elward*
Mr. H. Hal Garner and Dr. Harold Hawkins, *Evans-Bontura*
The National Park Service, *Mount Locust*
Ms. Camile Butler, *Myrtle Terrace*
Rev. Matthew Covington, *The Presbyterian Manse*
Mrs. Helen Spencer, *Marschalk House*
Dr. and Mrs. Ken Stubbs, *Riverview*
Mr. Arthur LaSalle, *Springfield*
Mr. and Mrs. Joe Meng, *Wigwam*
Ms. Shirley Petkovsek, *Griffith-McComas House*
Mr. and Mrs. Phillip Smith, *The John Smith House*
Mississippi Department of Archives and History, *Historic Jefferson Military College*

WELCOME TO NATCHEZ

Chivalry and romance, grandeur and wealth, adventure, passion, and power—this is Natchez.

Listen for the echoes of Aaron Burr's whispered intrigues and the laughter and song of Lafayette's jubilant soirees. Discover the sunken roads upon which Andrew Jackson marched to battle or quietly strolled in courtship. Look through the early-morning fog on a Vidalia sandbar for the ghosts of proud gentlemen, pistols in hand, risking their lives in defense of honor.

Walk the tree-lined streets of architectural treasures and be refreshed in the long shadows of great white pillars. Enjoy the legendary Southern cuisine and incomparable hospitality. Finally, gaze upon the mighty Mississippi River, so intimately tied to the fortunes of antebellum Natchez, a silent witness to the colorful history of this, its oldest settlement.

At every turn, Natchez will charm and delight you—and remain forever in your memory.

NATCHEZ UNDER FIVE FLAGS

Rising majestically more than two hundred feet above the mighty Mississippi, the Bluffs of Natchez have drawn to their heights countless generations seeking a haven of safety and a promise of prosperity.

Long before the first European settlers arrived, the Natchez Indians hunted buffalo and worshiped their gods. They surrendered their sacred hunting grounds only after these serene cliffs had been drenched in blood.

In 1682 the French explorer La Salle sailed in search of the mouth of the Mississippi. The first European to recognize the strategic value of the cliffs, La Salle understood that whoever controlled these heights controlled the river. In 1716 Bienville erected Ft. Rosalie to further secure the interests of Louis XV's France.

For more than a decade the French and the Natchez Indians peacefully shared the bluffs. But in 1729 tragedy struck. The French commander tried to occupy a sacred Indian village. The Indians, in turn, attacked the royal garrison, killing virtually everyone. Three years later, the French returned and all but annihilated the Indian population. Despite this, the French hold on the region was already slipping.

In 1763, at the close of the French and Indian War, the British raised their Union Jack over Ft. Rosalie. The British Crown offered sizeable land grants to encourage settlement and expand its influence. The British laid out a small town at Natchez landing—now called Natchez-Under-the-Hill. By the time of the American Revolution, the number of successful English Loyalists had grown significantly.

An unsuccessful raid on Natchez in 1778 by American revolutionary James Willing indicated to the Spanish governor of Louisiana just how vulnerable was the British hold on the area. In 1779 Spain declared war against England; and while George III was trying to suppress the American rebellion on the eastern seaboard, Spain quietly dominated Natchez. Adopting an attitude of benign rule over their newest territory, the Spanish offered larger land grants than the British, ushering in an even greater prosperity for the region. Though Natchez customs and manners remained largely Anglo-Saxon, the architecture began to reflect a Latin influence. Between 1787 and 1791 the Spanish laid out the present town on the bluff.

Once the Revolution was over, the newly independent Americans were free to travel south and westward. Pinckney's Treaty of 1795 ceded to America the east bank of the Mississippi River. In 1797 Andrew Ellicott raised the American flag in full view of the Spanish fort. By 1798 the dons of Natchez gave up their control and, as part of the Mississippi Territory, Natchez became an American town. The 1801 treaty with the remaining Indian tribes opened the Natchez Trace to wagon travel and mail delivery and brought a period of intense American settlement. By 1811 the first steamboat had docked at the wharves Under-the-Hill. The reign of "King Cotton" had begun, bringing with it fifty years of extraordinary prosperity and abundance. By 1830 only New York City had more millionaires than Natchez.

During the Civil War, Natchez was occupied by Federal troops. However, the city had no railroad connections and was regarded as having little importance. Thus, except for a few Union gunboat shellings, Natchez was spared the incendiary ravages of war. Following Appomattox, Natchez again looked to the Mississippi River and the surrounding fertile soil for its future prosperity. However, the country had changed dramatically. New and expanding railway systems rendered the great steamboats obsolete. Natchez was stranded in the midst of its decaying cotton fields and family fortunes.

Because Natchez did not share in the prosperity that came to the rest of the country, it could not afford to tear down its old landmarks to make way for the newly fashionable Victorian gingerbread architecture. Throughout the Reconstruction era and much of the later Great Depression, Natchez could only cling to its elegant past. Thus, an invaluable treasury of America's architectural heritage—more than three hundred antebellum structures—was saved from destruction or wholesale renovation. In the words of William C. Allen, "Fortune conspired to leave us precious few places that speak of history as clearly and eloquently as Natchez. Here a tidy merchant-class town center is surrounded on three sides by magnificent suburban estates which together form a highly concentrated and well preserved slice of nineteenth-century life in the American South."

Today, Natchez is cited as a paradigm of sensible and humane small-town planning by proponents of the "New Urbanism," the growing movement in urban design seeking to replace suburban sprawl with enduring and meaningful communities.

THE NATCHEZ PILGRIMAGE

In 1932 a small group of visionary Natchez women sought to share their town's rich heritage with the rest of the world. Through their efforts the Natchez Pilgrimage was born—and with it, a new and exciting era in the history of Natchez.

Today, pioneer families—and new owners as well—open the doors of their historic houses to more than 150,000 visitors a year. They join the ranks of such distinguished Natchez guests as Andrew Jackson, the Marquis de Lafayette, Jim Bowie, Zachary Taylor, Mark Twain, Jefferson Davis, William Dunbar, John James Audubon, Stephen Foster, William Howard Taft, Jenny Lind, Henry Clay, Mrs. Woodrow Wilson, Mrs. Franklin Delano Roosevelt, Gen. Douglas MacArthur, Piet Maar, and Mrs. Lyndon Johnson.

The highlight of these month-long pilgrimages—now the largest in America—is the Confederate Pageant. With its king, queen, court, tableaux groups, and dancers— all in lavish antebellum dress—the pageant seeks to briefly turn back the clock to the courtly days and charm of Natchez's gracious past. It fosters an appreciation for what was truly best in that great heritage: a respect for the strength of the family and the value of a genteel existence with its emphasis on cordiality, chivalry, culture, and honor. Information on the Pilgrimage may be obtained by calling (800) 647-6742.

THE HISTORIC NATCHEZ FOUNDATION

The Historic Natchez Foundation, founded in 1974 by Ron and Mimi Miller, is a nonprofit organization dedicated to the preservation and enhancement of those Natchez buildings and neighborhoods important to the future of the Natchez region and our national heritage. Since its inception in 1964, the foundation has been instrumental in revitalizing the Natchez commercial center and has provided financial incentives for the rehabilitation of smaller historic properties in neighborhoods placed by the foundation on the National Register of Historic Places. Today, the foundation is finding financially feasible uses for buildings threatened with demolition. It is working with the city to improve the state and local preservation ordinances so that they can better function with the new Natchez Historical Park.

The foundation spearheaded streetscape-beautification programs that included sidewalk paving and tree planting. It initiated a successful program to research the nationally important African-American history of the Natchez area. Natchez has now become a pioneer in African-American heritage tourism. With the creation of the Center for the Conservation of Decorative Arts, the foundation expanded its preservation efforts to include the material culture and decorative arts of Natchez and the southeastern United States. More information may be obtained by calling (601) 442-2500.

CONTENTS

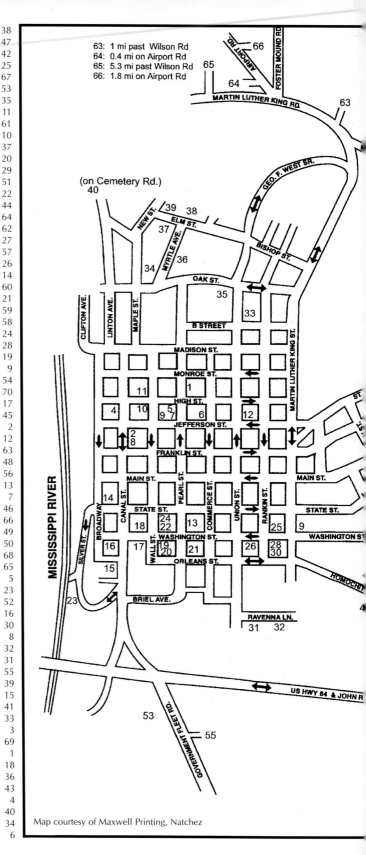

63: 1 mi past Wilson Rd
64: 0.4 mi on Airport Rd
65: 5.3 mi past Wilson Rd
66: 1.8 mi on Airport Rd

(on Cemetery Rd.)

Map courtesy of Maxwell Printing, Natchez

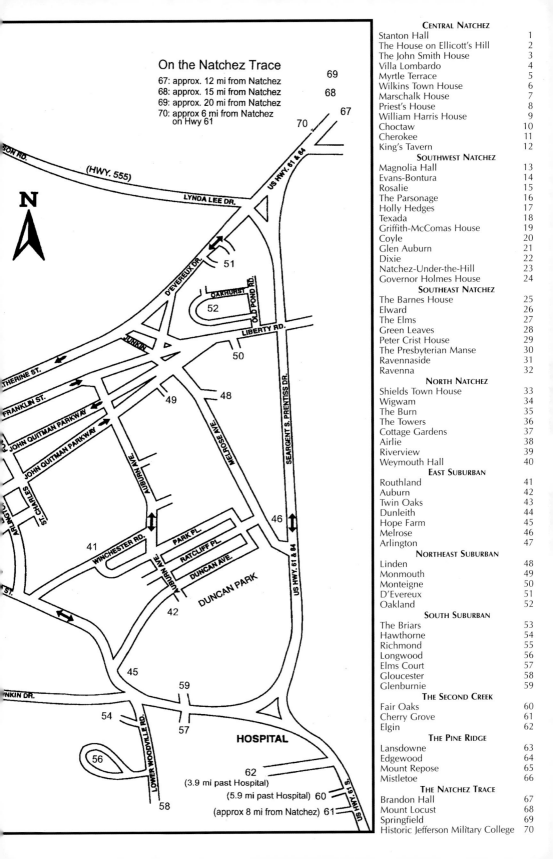

On the Natchez Trace

67: approx. 12 mi from Natchez
68: approx. 15 mi from Natchez
69: approx. 20 mi from Natchez
70: approx 6 mi from Natchez
on Hwy 61

STANTON HALL
1857, National Historic Landmark

In 1851 Frederick Stanton, a planter and cotton merchant of Irish origin, began work on his palatial town house mansion. Originally called *Belfast,* it was completed in 1857, just prior to the onset of the Civil War. Stanton died only two years later, but his family remained at *Stanton Hall* until 1894.

For his princely residence, Stanton sent his architect and contractor, Thomas Rose, to Europe to select the finest appointments available. These included English sterling-silver doorknobs and Sheffield hinges, mantlepieces of Italian Carrara marble, rose-patterned iron for the balconies, French pier and over-mantle mirrors, and great bronze chandeliers. Rose chartered an entire sailing ship to bring this treasury of European craftsmanship to Natchez. Stanton is reported to have paid the then-incredible sum of $83,300 to build his *Belfast*. Significantly, *Stanton Hall* was totally built by local artisans.

Like other great houses built just before the Civil War, *Stanton Hall* is of Greek Revival design. It is augmented with such Victorian and Italianate ornaments as the brackets and arched openings of the observatory and the lacy ironwork of the projecting side bays. The extraordinary interiors include an unusual arrangement of three parlors

separated by sliding doors or hanging arches, a seventeen-foot-high entrance hall-way, rosewood furnishings with priceless silver accents, and gasoliers similar to those in the United States Treasury Building.

During the Civil War, a portion of one of the pillars was blasted by a Union gunboat, and Union troops were housed in the servants' quarters. Reconstruction also was a time of hardship. During the 1890s the mansion was home to the Stanton College for Young Ladies and the name was changed to *Stanton Hall*. At one point, the First Bank of Natchez auctioned the mansion for a price less than the cost of the iron fence.

In 1938 Stanton Hall was purchased by the Pilgrimage Garden Club, which now operates it as one of America's finest house museums. Occupying an entire city block in the heart of Natchez, the landscaped grounds feature century-old oaks. The Carriage House Restaurant and Lounge specializes in Southern fried chicken and mint juleps.

OPPOSITE: This bedroom is one of six that have been restored.
ABOVE: The parlor features massive pier mirrors (the largest in Natchez), marble mantle-pieces, and Cornelius Baker gasoliers.

THE HOUSE ON ELLICOTT'S HILL
1797, National Historic Landmark

When Natchez was still a Spanish territory governed by Don Manuel Gayoso de Lemos, this hill, with its commanding view of the bluff and the river, was vacant and belonged to the Spanish Crown. Don Manuel married an American in 1775 and presented this land to his mother-in-law, Frances Ashton Watts.

With the 1795 Treaty of San Lorenzo, Spain ceded lands north of the thirty-first parallel to the new United States. The Spanish dons, of course, were still reluctant to leave. In 1797 Maj. Andrew Ellicott, an American surveyor, was ordered to occupy the land and raise the American flag in defiance of the Spanish who could see it from their positions at Ft. Rosalie. The Spanish eventually left in 1798, and it is from this episode that the hill takes its name.

In 1797 the property was acquired by merchant James Moore, who is believed to have built the existing house. Nearby was a tavern operated by Patrick Connelly, and for years this house was mistakenly thought to be that tavern. In fact, the house is a combination residence above and business below.

It was purchased by Dr. Frederick Seip in 1816. From 1849 to 1878 the house and its

outbuildings became The Natchez High School for Boys. After serving as worker housing for the cotton mills, the building rapidly deteriorated. Restoration of the house by the Natchez Garden Club began in the 1930s. Supervised by the architectural firm of Koch and Wilson, it was the first building restoration project undertaken by a Natchez organization.

The West Indies-inspired design features a double-tiered front gallery, colonnettes on pedestals, and surrounding shed roofs attached to a central gabled roof. The interiors are from the Moore and Seip inventories.

OPPOSITE, BELOW: Unusual wooden drawbridges connected to the second story were raised at night to protect against outlaws.
ABOVE: The original dining room is pictured here.
BELOW: The original kitchen shown here dates to 1798.

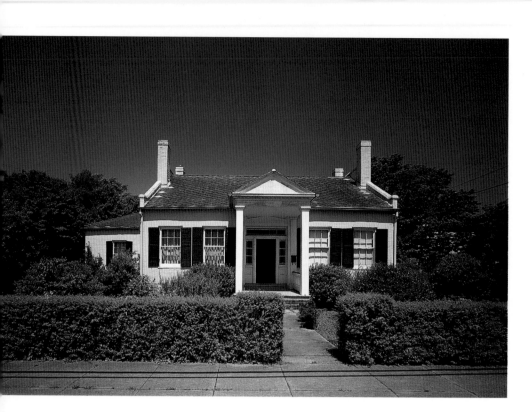

THE JOHN SMITH HOUSE
1837

John Smith, a superintendent for and later a partner in the Neibert and Gemmell construction firm, designed and built this charming house in 1837. Smith and his partners were heavily invested in local real estate, and the firm was financially ruined by the recession of 1837. The house was sold at auction. In 1841 a brutal tornado struck Natchez, killing Smith.

VILLA LOMBARDO
late 1800s

Located at the point where the Old Trace turned south along the river, *Villa Lombardo* has had a colorful and at times infamous history. Peepholes in the interior doors suggest it first served as a house of prostitution. It later became a residence, and then the location of Ellicott's Inn, a restaurant run by the Natchez Garden Club. From the late 1950s until only recently, it housed the antique collection of John Lombardo. Now vacant, this beautifully proportioned brick building with its magnificent iron gateway awaits its next role.

This iron gateway is unique in Natchez.

MYRTLE TERRACE
1851

This serene house was once owned by the legendary 270-pound Capt. Tom Leathers, who piloted the *Natchez* against the *Robert E. Lee* in 1870 in the historic $20,000 winner-take-all race immortalized by Currier and Ives. The race from New Orleans to St. Louis drew international attention and high-stakes betting. In the end, Leathers idled for six hours in a fog bank to protect his passengers and lost the race. This giant of a man was ultimately run down by a bicyclist and died from his injuries.

Shaped like a regional cottage, with a large gable roof shading deep galleries, *Myrtle Terrace* is named for the abundant crepe myrtle trees in the front yard. The slender columns are a typical Federal-style detail and contrast with the Gothic cast-iron fence.

MARSCHALK HOUSE *(RIGHT)*
1796

Andrew Marschalk, Mississippi's first printer, presented this beautiful cottage on elegant North Pearl Street to his daughter, Jane Elenore, as a wedding present. It has been remodeled several times since then. Helen Spencer, its present owner, has added an exquisite English garden in the back, designed by landscape architect William Garbo.

THE WILKINS TOWN HOUSE
1835

This modest Greek Revival brick town house features a gabled roof with parapet end walls, each with a pair of chimneys linked by a curtain wall. It rests on a fully raised basement and has a two-tiered, full-width rear gallery. Once the Natchez-Adams County Chamber of Commerce, it is now an antique store.

PRIEST'S HOUSE
circa 1783

Originally located on Market Street, the *Priest's House* was moved to North Canal, next to *The House on Ellicott's Hill*, as part of a Natchez Garden Club restoration project. During Spanish rule, a beloved Catholic padre named Father Lennan lived here for more than fifteen years. In March of 1798 the Spanish folded their flags and left Ft. Rosalie. On March 27, realizing the Spanish were gone for good, Lennan sold his house, the first in Natchez to change hands under the new American regime. Next door is the law office of Judge Winchester, who oversaw the education of Jefferson Davis's second bride, Varina Howell.

WILLIAM HARRIS HOUSE
circa 1835

This imposing two-story house was built by William Harris, an early planter, civic leader, and father of Confederate Gen. Nathaniel Harrison Harris. During the time he lived here, Harris was building *Ravenna* as his family home. In 1851 *Harris House* was purchased by Nathaniel Loomis Carpenter, who sold *Myrtle Terrace* to Capt. Tom Leathers. Carpenter, a successful builder and contractor, was the patriarch of one of Natchez's most philanthropic families. He no doubt supervised the 1855 renovations to the exterior. The Carpenters sold the *Harris House* in 1886 and moved to *Dunleith*, which became their family home for five generations.

CHOCTAW
1836, National Register of Historic Places

Built as a town house for contractor and real-estate investor Joseph Niebert, *Choctaw* is thought to have been designed by architect/builder James Hardie. In 1844 it became the home of planter/philanthropist Alvarez Fisk, who deeded the property to the city for the Natchez Institute, the first totally free Mississippi public school.

With its Indian cross-sticks-of-war baluster decoration, *Choctaw* was built at the time when styles were changing from Federal to Greek Revival. The portico, with its Roman Ionic columns and oval light in the pediment, is Federal. The entrance doorway and interior millwork are Greek Revival. The columns at street level and the double entrance are reminiscent of the great houses of the Charleston Battery.

CHEROKEE
circa 1794

Convinced that the source of the dreaded yellow fever was found below ground, the Spanish officials of the times passed an ordinance prohibiting excavations within the city. Consequently, Jesse Greenfield built *Cherokee* on the crown of the hill, allowing the rear of the house to follow the natural contour of the land. The result is one of the truly unique houses of Natchez.

Cherokee served as the first American soldier encampment in 1798, when Natchez was claimed for the United States. After this period, the dates and sequence of alterations to this unusual house are not exactly known. The evolution of its design may involve an extensive remodeling, or it could have been built anew after the introduction of Greek Revival to Natchez in the early 1830s. It is thought that in 1811 owner David Michie built the Levi Weeks-designed Greek temple portico that is recessed between the two small "cabinet rooms." *Cherokee* sustained damage in the tornado of 1841 and again might have been either remodeled or built anew. *Cherokee* was purchased in 1846 by land baron Frederick Stanton, who lived there until 1858, when he moved to his palatial *Stanton Hall*.

KING'S TAVERN

circa 1789, National Register of Historic Places

King's Tavern is believed to be the oldest building in Natchez—some say in all of Mississippi. The first U.S. mail to reach Natchez, brought over the Natchez Trace by an Indian runner, was delivered here. The tavern was a welcome stopping place for denizens of the Natchez Trace: Ohio flatboatmen, Tennessee backwoodsmen, Eastern traders, river pirates, and highwaymen from everywhere.

Resembling a pre-Revolutionary war blockhouse, *King's Tavern* features a steeply pitched roof, the original beaded clapboards, and exposed beaded beams in the original room on the main floor. It is a two-story house, one room deep and one room wide, with a one-story shed-roof porch at the front and rear. The tavern, restored in the early 1970s by the Pilgrimage Garden Club, now functions once more as a tavern and restaurant. Visitors can still see the scattered bullet holes left by an early Indian attack.

MAGNOLIA HALL (*OPPOSITE*)

1858, National Register of Historic Places

Thomas Henderson, a Natchez native, was a wealthy cotton broker and merchant. He began *Magnolia Hall* in 1858 on the site of the Henderson Family house, Pleasant Hill, which was moved to accommodate the new mansion.

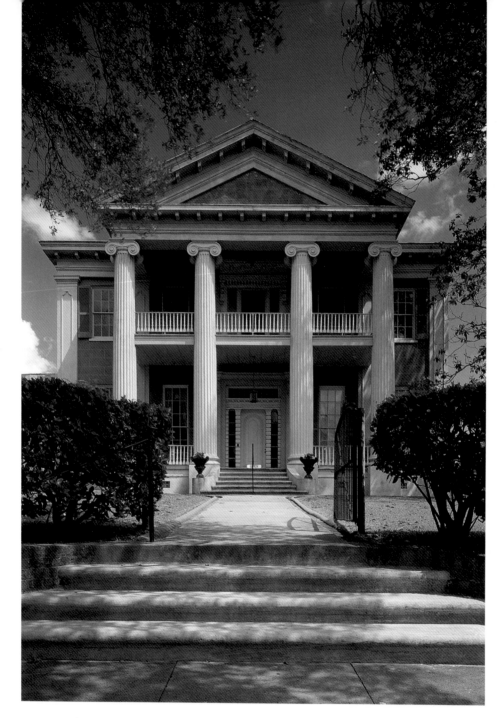

Magnolia Hall was named for the painted magnolia blossoms in the parlor ceiling's centerpieces. The stucco is painted a brownstone red, reminiscent of the building materials then popular in the Northeast, and is scored to simulate mortar.

A splendid example of Greek Revival architecture, *Magnolia Hall* was one of the last great mansions built prior to the Civil War.

EVANS-BONTURA
circa 1850, National Register of Historic Places

In the early 1850s Robert Smith, a free black businessman, built what was then a simple, unadorned brick town house overlooking the Mississippi. Almost half of the free black citizens of Mississippi lived in Natchez. The two-story rear carriage house features wide arches for the carriages Smith used in his taxi business.

The subsequent owner, Joseph Bontura, was a Portuguese-born wine merchant. In 1860 Bontura is thought to have added the two-story brick wing that connects the carriage house to the main house. He used the carriage house and stables for his own horses and adapted the house for use as an inn. Bontura also is thought to have added the cast-iron balconies that give *Evans-Bontura* its Latin flavor. It is from these balconies, no doubt, that many watched the great *Natchez-Robert E. Lee* steamboat race.

Years later the house was purchased by Mr. and Mrs. Hugh Evans. Mrs. Evans was the coauthor of the romantic histories *They Found It In Natchez* and *A Day In Natchez*. Notables such as Stephen Foster and Mark Twain were entertained in the banquet hall at *Evans-Bontura*. In the front bedroom stood the bed used by Scarlet O'Hara in the filming of *Gone with the Wind*.

For a time, *Evans-Bontura* was run as a museum house by the National Society of the Colonial Dames of America in the State of Mississippi. Now it is again in private hands, under the ownership of H. Hal Garner and Dr. Harold Hawkins.

An air of mystery has always pervaded *Evans-Bontura*. Some claim the ghost of Mark Twain still visits the house, moving items of furniture and unhinging mirrors from the walls. Others still wonder about what lies at the foot of the descending stairs that lead to a long-since closed-off cellar.

TOP: *Stephen Foster, Mark Twain, and other notables all dined at Evans-Bontura.*

ABOVE AND RIGHT: *Both Robert Smith and Joseph Bontura kept their stables in the Carriage Wing.*

ROSALIE
1823, National Historic Landmark

One of this nation's great mansions, *Rosalie* was named for the nearby French Ft. Rosalie, which itself was named after the Duchess of Pontchartrain. *Rosalie* was the dream house of Pennsylvanian Peter Little and his wife, Eliza. Little owned a cotton plantation in Louisiana and built the first steam-powered lumbermill on the Mississippi. Having made his fortune, he was eager join Natchez society. However,

Eliza, a childhood convert of the evangelist Lorenzo Dow, reportedly used *Rosalie* as a rest stop for itinerant Methodist preachers. Peter built *The Parsonage* in 1840 as a separate haven for her minister friends.

The Littles, who lived at *Rosalie* for sixteen years, died without an heir. In 1857 the mansion was purchased by the Andrew Wilson family. During their residency the house underwent extensive interior renovation and redecoration, including the addition of elaborate plasterwork, marble mantlepieces, over-mantle gilt mirrors,

and an eighteen-piece Belter parlor set whose pattern is now referred to by historians as the "Rosalie" pattern. The Wilson furnishings have remained at Rosalie.

When Natchez fell to Union forces, *Rosalie* was used as a Federal headquarters. It was first occupied by Gen. U. S. Grant, followed by Gen. Walter Q. Gresham, who actually became friends of the Wilsons. Wilson family members lived at *Rosalie* until 1938, when the house was sold to the Mississippi State Society Daughters of the American Revolution. The society operates *Rosalie* as a museum house and in 1972 bought the original adjacent four-acre garden. From its commanding location, *Rosalie* overlooks the Mississippi to the west and the Spanish promenade along the bluffs to the north.

Rosalie is a hip-roofed, two-story brick structure with two-story-high columns supporting a portico that covers both the three central openings of the front facade and a full-width gallery across the rear. The widely admired antique cypress picket fence contains no nails in its structure. Thought to have been designed by Baltimore architect James Shryach Griffin, *Rosalie* established an architectural form for the great houses of Natchez and for plantation houses throughout the South.

ABOVE: The double parlors feature a complete set of Belter rosewood furniture and gold-leaf mirrors hidden from Federal troops during the Civil War.
OPPOSITE, ABOVE: This remarkably preserved child's bedroom and its furnishings all date from antebellum times.
OPPOSITE, BELOW: The canopied four-poster bed was used by Gen. U. S. Grant during a visit to the Union headquarters at Rosalie.

THE PARSONAGE
1852

ABOVE: The rear gardens are extensively planted.
BELOW: The furnishings and china are all Metcalfe family heirlooms.

Peter Little donated to the Methodist Episcopal Church a piece of land adjacent to his mansion *Rosalie*. His intention was to provide a retreat for the itinerant minister friends of his wife, Eliza, a convert of pioneer evangelist Lorenzo Dow.

The Parsonage was designed by James Hardie, a Scottish immigrant and superintendent of construction for Neibert and Gemmell. It is a Greek Revival house raised on a full basement to provide a view over the bluff to the river below. The back porch connects with the gallery of an elongated post-Civil War wing that encloses one side of the back yard.

The Methodist Church sold *The Parsonage* in 1865. In 1893 it was purchased by Mrs. James Metcalfe, and her descendants have carefully preserved *The Parsonage* to this day.

HOLLY HEDGES
1796

John Scott, a carpenter at the Spanish fort, was given a land grant in the heart of Old Spanish Natchez by the Spanish governor with the unusual stipulation that no bullfighting could take place in his side yard. There is still some debate about the actual house now standing on this land. It might well be the house Scott built in 1796, or it might be one built around 1818, when the property was acquired by Edward Turner. Turner was the mayor of Natchez from 1815-19 and served Mississippi as a state attorney, speaker of its House of Representatives, and chief justice of its Supreme Court.

In 1832 Turner gave the house as a wedding present to his daughter, Mary, who married John McMurran, a law partner and brother-in-law of Gen. John Quitman. The McMurrans added many of the Greek Revival-inspired elements seen today. They lived at *Holly Hedges* until their expanded fortunes allowed them to build palatial *Melrose*.

Following the McMurrans, *Holly Hedges* had many owners, including Fanny Bontura, widow of Portuguese wine merchant Joseph Bontura. In 1948 it was completely restored by Mr. and Mrs. Earl Hart Miller. *Holly Hedges* is entered at street level through a Federal-style doorway with an elliptical fanlight. The two dormers were added in 1950.

TEXADA
1793, National Register of Historic Places

Although the exact date of the house's construction is not certain, it is known that the Spanish government granted this lot in the old Spanish Quarter to Michael Solibellas in 1793. When it was sold to Manuel Texada in 1793, the lot had a house fifty feet by thirty feet, including galleries. It is thought to be the first brick building in Natchez. In 1817 it was sold to Edward Turner, the mayor of Natchez from 1815-19, Mississippi state attorney, speaker of the state House of Representatives, and chief justice of the state Supreme Court. Before the state capital moved from Natchez, the state legislature met here. *Texada* also was the home of Mr. Haughten's Dancing Academy (1806) and the American Eagle Tavern.

Texada was remodeled in the mid-nineteenth century and, more recently, by Dr. and Mrs. George W. Moss.

GRIFFITH-McCOMAS HOUSE *(OPPOSITE)*
circa 1794

The second story of this West Indies-inspired house was the "tenement house" that stood on this site in 1818. It was built either by tailor Hugh Coyle, who owned the land from 1793-99, or by Leonard Pomet, a shopkeeper who owned the land from 1799-1807. Thus, as was common in Natchez, the original first story of this house was jacked up and placed on a new brick foundation. The present front gallery was built in the 1960s to replace the one lost to an earlier Victorian renovation. The symmetrical openings on the lower story are typical of the Federal style popular in Natchez from 1800-1836. Also typical of the style are the elliptical fanlights, sidelights, and four slender columns.

The house takes it name from William and John Griffith, founders of the Mississippi State Bar Association, who owned it from 1819-30 , and Anna McComas, a relative of George Washington and the widow of Gen. J. H. McComas. The general was once the mayor of Natchez and commander of a troop that welcomed Lafayette to the city in 1825. He also fought with his friend Andrew Jackson at the Battle of New Orleans. Among other owners of the house was the Reverend Daniel Smith, who organized Natchez's First Presbyterian Church in 1817.

The Griffith-McComas *dining room features excellent Federal-style woodwork.*

COYLE
1794

Irishman Hugh Coyle, one of the first tailors in Natchez, received a land grant from Governor Gayosa and built his house in the Spanish style using brick construction with a simple facade. It is quite similar to St. Augustine's "Oldest House in the U.S." In 1960 the Natchez Historical Society began restoration. Now it is again in private hands.

DIXIE
1853

There is still some doubt as to the earliest structures built on this lot. The rear dependency might have been built in 1795 by Maurice Stackpoole under a Spanish land grant. Samuel Davis, the brother of Jefferson Davis, also is thought to have built a house on this site. Reliable records indicate that in 1853 Edward Templeton began work on what is now *Dixie*. Although it is only a small brick cottage, the generous Greek Doric portico gave *Dixie* a monumental presence that prompted the city of Natchez to render—in Templeton's opinion—an overly high tax assessment. The small geometric garden is typical of Natchez antebellum town houses built close to the street.

When Templeton died, *Dixie* was put up for auction in 1855, apparently never having been occupied. Among its owners was the Bowie family, relatives of frontiersman Jim Bowie, whose famous knife was designed and fabricated in Natchez.

For years during this century, *Dixie* stood unoccupied and deteriorating, its rotting floors and ceilings open to the elements. Fortunately, this historic house has been saved by the extraordinary efforts of Mr. and Mrs. Tom Ketchings.

GLEN AUBURN *(LEFT)*
1875, National Register of Historic Places

Glen Auburn is a rare French Second Empire mansion in the middle of antebellum Natchez. This Victorian inn was recently restored and includes Eastlake-style chandeliers, extraordinary millwork and ornamental plaster, and period antiques in each room.

NATCHEZ-UNDER-THE-HILL
circa 1790, National Register of Historic Places

By 1790 *Natchez-Under-the-Hill* was already infamous for its bars, prostitutes, gamblers, and transient thugs. By the 1830s these elements had given way to warehouses and commercial establishments, but the neighborhood still retained some of its reputation. Run-down as recently as the 1960s, the area has made a remarkable comeback today with successful shops and restaurants, all with wonderful views of the river.

GOVERNOR HOLMES HOUSE *(LEFT)*
1794

Gov. David Holmes was the last governor of the Mississippi Territory and the first governor of the state of Mississippi. During that time his house, one of the oldest in Natchez, was the center of Natchez society. Jefferson Davis also was reported to have owned the house. Beautifully restored, it is now a popular bed-and-breakfast.

ELWARD
1844

Richard Elward was a bookbinder and a Natchez newspaper editor. His house is a beautifully proportioned Greek Revival brick cottage. It features gable-ended chimneys linked by a brick wall, and dormers trimmed with pilasters and cornices.

THE BARNES HOUSE
1830

This New England-flavored house was actually one of three prefabricated structures built in Ohio and shipped down the river by barge. Some of the interior hardware was locally made, including locks fabricated by L. Fitzpatrick, who forged the first Bowie knife.

THE ELMS
1804, National Register of Historic Places

The Elms is one of the earliest-documented houses in Natchez. Its builder, John Henderson, immigrated from Scotland in 1787 and wrote the first book published in the Natchez territory. He purchased the land in 1804, and when he sold it in 1810, he advertised the residence as "nearly new." The floor plan, low ceilings, thick walls, narrow window facings, and wide verandas all reflect Spanish influence.

The Elms was originally a Federal-style two-and-one-half-story brick structure with two rooms on each floor. The rear two-story gallery was soon enclosed, and double-tiered galleries were built to encircle the house. In the 1850s David Stanton, whose brother Frederick built *Stanton Hall,* added a two-story, Greek Revival stuccoed wing to the front porch and enclosed it to make an entrance hall. This alteration effectively changed the orientation of the house from south to west.

Other owners of *The Elms* have included the Reverend George Potts, a Presbyterian minister, and the first high sheriff of the Mississippi Territory.

GREEN LEAVES

1838, National Register of Historic Places

Built by George Fourniquet, this Greek Revival house with its noble Doric portico is one of the most richly detailed in Natchez. In 1849 it was purchased by George Koontz who, along with William and Audley Britton, founded the Britton and Koontz Bank, which is still a major financial institution in Natchez.

To this day, the descendants of George Koontz occupy *Green Leaves* and continue to carefully preserve its invaluable architectural details and Empire and Rocco Revival furnishings.

A monumental live oak dominates the rear courtyard.

PETER CRIST HOUSE
circa 1800

The slim columns and galleries reflect the West Indies influence seen throughout Natchez. In earlier guidebooks the house was referred to as *Ellislee*. To the rear is one of the few detached brick kitchens still in operation.

THE PRESBYTERIAN MANSE
1824-32, National Register of Historic Places

The Manse was built by Mrs. Margaret Overaker, the widow of George Overaker, who operated the White Horse Tavern and lived at *Hope Farm*. It was purchased in 1838 by the Presbyterian Church to be used as a parsonage. The Greek Revival building in the side yard was built in 1849 as a study for Rev. Joseph Buck Statton, minister of the church for fifty years and pastor emeritus until his death in 1903. *The Manse* is still the home of the ministers of the First Presbyterian Church.

RAVENNASIDE
circe 1830s, National Register of Historic Places

Ravennaside was built by Mr. and Mrs. James Fleming as a home for entertainment. Accordingly, *Ravennaside* was host to writers, publishers, architects, politicians, foreign dignitaries, and the elite of Natchez. Fleming's daughter, Mrs. Roane Fleming "Aweet Auntie" Byrnes, was famous for her work in the Natchez Trace Association, serving as its president from 1936 until her death in 1970. *Ravennaside* has been run as a guest house by its owners, Mr. and Mrs. John Van Hook, since 1973. Among its features is an extraordinary parquet floor in the Gold Room.

RAVENNA *(OPPOSITE)*
1835, National Register of Historic Places

Ravenna was one of the first Greek Revival houses in Natchez. It was built by the well-known contracting firm of Neibert and Gemmell for cotton merchant and developer William Harris. It is a typical Lower Mississippi Valley structure with double-tiered galleries recessed under the front and rear slopes of the gabled roof, supported by Doric columns on the first floor and Ionic on the second. This superimposition of orders exists elsewhere only at *Brandon Hall*. The dramatic hallway arch (*right*) is supported by paired Doric columns. The elliptical stairway is one the most beautiful in Natchez.

Among the owners of *Ravenna* were the Metcalfe family, one of whom, Zueleike, smuggled food to Confederate soldiers from the nearby bayou. Banished from *Ravenna* during the occupation, she eventually returned to her beloved home. Another kinsman, Dr. William Rousseau Cox, reportedly freed a prince, enslaved in Natchez, who had saved the life of his father, Dr. John Coates Cox, on one of the latter's Timbuktu expeditions.

Ravenna's *elliptical stairway and arches have a dramatic appearance.*

SHIELDS TOWN HOUSE
1860, National Register of Historic Places

Built by Delaware foundryman Maurice Lisle and his wife, Isabella (daughter of Natchez mayor John Stockman), this graceful Greek Revival cottage has beautiful Italianate details. It was sold to the Wilmer Shields family in 1869 and was called the *Shields Town House* to distinguish it from their country house on *Oakland Plantation*.

THE BURN
1836, National Register of Historic Places

At the age of twenty-one, John P. Walworth left his home in Cleveland, Ohio, and set off by steamboat for New Orleans. He stopped for shore leave in Natchez and never left. There he prospered as a planter and merchant, later becoming mayor of Natchez. His home, *The Burn*, is one of the earliest documented Greek Revival residences in Natchez.

Built by contractors Montgomery and Keyes, who also built structures at Jefferson College, it is named for the brook—*burn* in Scottish—that ran through the rear garden. The grand scale of the two-and-a-half-story house is masked by the cottagelike form. The exterior features paneled columns, fluted round columns on the central portico, and a splendid Greek Doric entablature.

During the Union occupation *The Burn* was used as a headquarters and hospital.

WIGWAM *(OPPOSITE, BELOW)*
1836

There is evidence that a structure stood on these grounds as early as the 1790s. In 1836 a portion of the *Cottage Gardens* property was sold to the four Ivy sisters. The Italianate front with projecting wings was built as an addition to the large cottage dating from 1836. Among its features are the arched triple windows, large central dormer, bracketed cornice, and cast-iron porch posts and railings. In 1858 the property was sold to Mr. Douglas Rivers and his wife, Eliza Little, the adopted daughter of the Littles of *Rosalie*. They named the house *Wigwam*, perhaps for the Indian burial ground thought to be on the site. Located within the boundaries of Ft. McPherson, the Union fortification, in northern Natchez, *Wigwam* was occupied by Union army officers during the Civil War.

Wigwam was restored in the 1960s by Dr. Harold C. Hawkins and H. Hal Garner.

THE TOWERS
circa 1859

Attorney and architect J. Edwards Smith created *The Towers* for W. C. Chamberlain, who bought the property with its existing frame cottage in 1859. Smith, who also built the Zion Chapel A.M.E. Church, added a new front and the two-story recessed porch with three arches on each floor set between the matching three-story towers that gave the house its name. The third stories were destroyed in a fire in 1927.

Mr. and Mrs. John Fleming bought the property in 1861. Like neighboring *Wigwam*, *The Towers* was within the Union fortification of Ft. McPherson and was occupied by Union officers.

COTTAGE GARDENS
circa 1830-40s, National Register of Historic Places

The property of *Cottage Gardens* may have been the center of a large royal land grant to Don Jose Vidal, whose estate reached the river and included what is now the National Cemetery and the site of the Charity Hospital. In 1798, with Natchez annexed by the United States, he was transferred to Post Concordia across the river.

The *Cottage Gardens* we now see was built in the 1830s or the 1840s, either as a complete remodeling of an existing house or as a totally new construction. Attorney Josephus Hewitt owned the property, which he called *Glen Home*, from 1845 to 1867. The Allison Foster family bought the house in 1884 and renamed it *Cottage Gardens*. Foster, a Union army officer, married a Natchez woman and became a beloved citizen of his adopted city.

Cottage Gardens is a story-and-a-half cottage with a Natchez-style gallery recessed under a gable roof with a triangular pediment. This particular combination of architectural elements is unique in Natchez. The original squared-off Greek Revival columns were replaced in the 1960s with round columns. The "sheaf-of-wheat" pattern railing connecting the columns is similar to that of *Choctaw*. The sunburst-pattern oval pediment window also is similar to that at *Choctaw*.

AIRLIE
circa 1790, National Register of Historic Places

Located on a high point in the northern part of town, *Airlie* is undoubtedly one of the earliest houses in Natchez. Its long, low, and narrow profile is typical of an early planter's cottage. Its many doors and windows provide for needed ventilation. *Airlie*'s architectural detailing suggests it was probably the "Mansion House" mentioned in the 1800s deed from Stephen (Don Esteban) Minor to new owner John Steele. Pennsylvanian Minor was an official for the Spanish government; Steele was a Revolutionary War colonel and later the governor of the Mississippi Territory. Steele renamed the house *Belvedere.*

The Aylette Buckner family purchased the property in 1832, renamed it *Airlie*, and extensively remodeled it. During the Civil War, *Airlie* was used as a Union hospital.

RIVERVIEW
circa 1841

Early records concerning the oldest portions of *Riverview* are vague, but some structure is thought to have stood on this site in northern Natchez before 1841. The property was owned by Spanish grandee Don Jose Vidal; Spanish government official Don Esteban Minor; and John Steele, the one-time governor of the Mississippi Territory who also owned *Airlie*.

The main portion of *Riverview* was built in 1869 by George M. Brown, an ex-Confederate lieutenant. Recalling the devastating tornado of 1841, Brown constructed his house with thirteen-inch-thick brick walls and anchored all the interior partitions to the foundation.

Recently restored by Dr. Harold C. Hawkins and H. Hal Garner, it is now owned by Dr. and Mrs. Ken Stubbs, who have continued to preserve the beauty of both the house and grounds.

The pond was part of a recent land-scaping plan for Riverview.

WEYMOUTH HALL
1855, National Register of Historic Places

Weymouth Hall was built by Judge Reuben Bullock and his wife, Sarah, niece of Mrs. John Weymouth. The Greek Revival house originally had a one-story gallery with a railed roof that encircled the house. Built on the edge of the high river bluff and upon an elevated basement, *Weymouth Hall* has perhaps the most dramatic vista of any residence in Natchez or the Mississippi River and its valley.

ROUTHLAND *(OPPOSITE TOP)*
1815-24, National Register of Historic Places

In 1790 Job Routh was granted a 180-acre tract by a Baron Carondelet. On a portion of this land, the present-day *Routhland* was built between 1815 and 1824 for Job's son, John Routh, and his wife, Nancy Smith. John Routh was one of the world's leading cotton planters. Originally a Federal-style cottage, it has undergone many remodelings and now has elements of Greek Revival and Italianate styles. The central portico was added in the mid-twentieth century.

Routhland is the third house to bear this name. The first *Routhland* was built in the late 1790s by Job Routh. It was destroyed by fire in 1855 and replaced by a second house, built for Routh's daughter, Mary, and her husband, Charles Dahlgren, on the same site. When the house was sold to Alfred Vidal Davis in 1859, he changed the name to *Dunleith,* and John Routh's home assumed the name *Routhland.* When the Routh family was caught in the Panic of 1837, *Routhland* was auctioned. In 1871 it was purchased by ex-Confederate Gen. Charles Clark, the Civil War governor of Mississippi.

The double parlors at Routhland feature Italianate detailing and are separated by fluted columns.

AUBURN
1812, National Historic Landmark

According to its architect, Levi Weeks, *Auburn* was the first house in the Territory on which any of the orders of classical architecture was ever attempted. *Auburn's* classical front portico and two-story columns became a model for mansions and

plantation houses throughout the South. Its portico predated those of the University of Virginia and the White House.

Auburn was designed for wealthy attorney and planter Lyman Harding, the first attorney general of the Mississippi Territory and later the state. In 1827 Auburn was purchased by Dr. Stephen Duncan, reportedly the world's largest cotton planter in

the 1850s. Duncan added the side wings, a service building, and a templelike billiard hall in the side yard. *Auburn* was host to such notables as Henry Clay, Edward Everett Hale, and John Howard Payne, the composer of "Home Sweet Home." In 1911 Duncan's heirs deeded *Auburn* and its 210 acres to the city of Natchez, stipulating that the recreational facilities were to be available to the public free of charge

Since 1972, *Auburn* has been run as a museum house by the Auburn Garden Club.

The interiors of Auburn *feature original furnishings and an extraordinary freestanding geometric stairway that is an architectural masterpiece.*

TWIN OAKS
1852, National Register of Historic Places

Charles Dubbuissen was a New Yorker who came to Natchez in the 1830s to be a professor at Jefferson College, the first state-chartered institution of higher learning. In 1835 he became the school's president. Dubbuissen also was an attorney and became a judge of the probate court.

Contractors Thomas Bowen and John Crouthers, who also built *Dunleith* and other Greek Revival buildings in Natchez, built *Twin Oaks* for Dubbuissen in 1852. The graceful story-and-a-half house features a templelike portico, square columns, and dormer windows to light the upper half-story.

Among the owners of *Twin Oaks* were the Reverend Pierce Connelly and his wife, Cornelia. After embracing the Catholic faith, Cornelia (Mother Connelly) founded a new order in England. The small chapel in the rear garden was dedicated to her. The current owners, the Whittingtons, extensively restored *Twin Oaks*.

DUNLEITH
1856, National Historic Landmark

Dunleith was built in 1856 by Charles Dahlgren, the son-in-law of Job Routh and a direct descendant of Sweden's King Gustavus Adolphus. Then called *Routhland,* it was built on the site of Routh family patriarch Job Routh's first *Routhland,* which was destroyed by fire in 1845. It was given the name *Dunleith* by its second owner, Alfred Vidal Davis, who bought it in 1859. The great house passed into the hands of "cotton king" and philanthropist Joseph Carpenter, and five generations of his family made *Dunleith* their home.

Contractor John Crouthers, a Maryland native, built *Dunleith* at the edge of a forty-acre landscaped park, part of Job Routh's original seventeen-hundred-acre

land grant from the Spanish government. To the basic Greek Revival style he added many Italianate details. *Dunleith* is the only house in Mississippi with a colonnade that completely surrounds the house.

The outbuildings at *Dunleith*, several of which are Gothic-inspired, are typical of an antebellum suburban estate and include a three-story service wing, a two-story poultry house, a two-story carriage house and stable, and an original garden hothouse.

Dunleith was used as the backdrop for the films *Huckleberry Finn* and *Showboat*. In 1976 it was restored under the direction of new owner William F. Heins III. The lower floor is open to the public. The second floor now serves as a bed-and-breakfast.

HOPE FARM
1775-89, National Register of Historic Places

The rear portion of *Hope Farm,* with its two-story veranda, was built in 1775 by Marcus Hoiler. The front portion was added around 1779 by Don Carlos de Gran Pre, the commandant of the Natchez District from 1780-92. Don Carlos was responsible for the plan of the town of Natchez. The Spanish influence is seen in the low overhangs and stuccoed wall of the deep front gallery.

In 1805 *Hope Farm* and its fifteen-acre grounds were purchased by George Overaker, a merchant and owner of the White Horse Tavern. From 1835 to 1926 *Hope Farm* was owned by the Montgomery family, who gave it its Greek Revival character. In 1927 *Hope Farm* was purchased by J. Balfour and Catherine Grafton Miller. Mrs. Miller is credited with founding the Natchez Pilgrimage, one of the first organized house tours in the United States. Today, Ethel Green Banta has lovingly maintained *Hope Farm* as both her residence and a bed-and-breakfast.

TOP: *Among the* Hope Farm *treasures in the living room are a portrait of Catherine Grafton Miller and a six-octave nineteenth-century piano.*
ABOVE: *In the rear is an antique kitchen with an Indian figurehead from the steamboat* Natchez.

MELROSE
circa 1845, National Historic Landmark

Melrose is one of the best-preserved and most significant historic houses in America. Along with its furnishings, grounds, and outbuildings, it is maintained in museum quality by the National Park Service. *Melrose* was designed and built in the Greek Revival style around 1845 by Natchez architect Jacob Beyers for attorney and Pennsylvania native John T. McMurran. It was named for the Scottish abbey immortalized by Sir Walter Scott.

After a series of financial and personal tragedies, McMurran sold *Melrose* in 1865 to Elizabeth Davis, wife of attorney George Malin Davis. They used the mansion

only occasionally, and in 1887 it was inherited by their daughter, Julia Davis Kelly, and her husband, Stephen Kelly. In 1901 the Kelly's son, George M. D. Kelly (who inherited *Melrose* along with *Choctaw*, *Cherokee*, and several other Natchez mansions), came to *Melrose* with his wife, Ethel. Enchanted with the estate, they made it their permanent residence and completely restored it. When Mrs. Kelly died in 1975, *Melrose* was sold intact with all the original furnishings to Mr. and Mrs. John Callon. In 1990 the Callons sold *Melrose* to the National Park Service.

Because of the succession of forward-thinking and sensitive owners, *Melrose* has come to us virtually intact as one of the finest examples of antebellum architecture in America.

ABOVE: *The furnishings in the drawing room are maintained in museum-quality condition.*

BELOW, LEFT: *Above the piano in the parlor is the funerary portrait of George Malin Davis's daughter, Francis, who died at age four.*

BELOW, RIGHT: *The solid mahogany punkah in the dining room is one of the most elaborate and best preserved in Natchez.*

OPPOSITE: *Ionic columns frame the view from the parlor into the drawing room.*

ARLINGTON
1818, National Historic Landmark

Arlington was built for Jane Surget, the daughter of French-born land baron Pierre Surget, who also built *Cherry Grove.* Her husband, John Hampton White, designed the first bank building in Mississippi. Ironically, John White died in 1819, Jane in 1825.

Arlington is a highly embellished Federal-style mansion. It features geometric curves, patterned brick work, a hand-carved wooden cornice, and marble trim around the windows and doors.

LINDEN
circa 1785, 1818, National Register of Historic Places

There is sketchy evidence that the two-story middle section of *Linden* was built in 1785. However, it is more likely that this first section was built in 1818 for Thomas B. Reed, one of Mississippi's first United States senators. Reed sold the property, which he called *Reedland*, to Dr. John Kerr, who added the wings on either side and the long ninety-eight-foot gallery. The two-story brick wing was added by Jane Conner, who bought *Linden* in 1849.

MONMOUTH
1818, National Historic Landmark

Monumental and commanding, *Monmouth* was built by John Hankinson and named for his native Monmouth County in New Jersey. Its best-known owner, however, was John A. Quitman, army general and commander in the Mexican War, state governor in 1849, and two-term member of Congress from 1855 on. Quitman remodeled *Monmouth* in 1853, choosing a powerful interpretation of the Greek Revival style. *Monmouth's* interior details still reflect its original Federal style. Quitman covered the original brick with scored stucco, added the large portico, the massive square columns, and broad zigzag railing. With Cincinnati architect James McClure, he added an east wing with a two-story gallery that wraps around the back of the house. Sadly, this great historical figure succumbed to food poisoning (or a version of legionnaires' disease) that he contracted at a banquet for President James Buchanan. Quitman died at *Monmouth* in 1858.

MONTEIGNE
1855, National Register of Historic Places

Monteigne was originally designed and built as an Italianate cottage by architect James McClure for William T. Martin, district attorney and husband of *Linden*'s Margaret Dunlop Conner. The name *Monteigne* and its original chalet-style design reflected Martin's French Huguenot lineage. As a Confederate general, Martin served with Jeb Stuart and Joe Wheeler. During the war *Monteigne* suffered under Union occupation.

In 1927 *Monteigne* was completely remodeled in neoclassical style by New Orleans architects Weiss, Dreyfus & Seiferth. The interior detailing still reflects the 1850s Italianate design.

The staircase dates from 1927; the original doorway moldings are from 1855.

D'EVEREUX

1836, National Register of Historic Places

Wealthy planter and philanthropist William St. John Elliott built *D'Evereux* on an eighty-acre tract alongside the Natchez Trace. It is named for Elliott's uncle, Gen. John D'Evereux, who served with Simon Bolivar. Elliott's good friend, Sen. Henry Clay of Kentucky, was a frequent visitor. During one stay, his portrait was painted by the French artist Bahin, and a legendary ball was held in his honor.

Designed by architect and builder James Hardie, *D'Evereux* is considered one of the hallmarks of the Greek Revival architecture but also has such elements of the Federal style as the fanlighted rear doorways. *D'Evereux* was used as the backdrop for the movie *The Heart of Maryland.*

Notables such as Henry Clay were entertained in this dining room.

OAKLAND
1838, National Register of Historic Places

After graduating Harvard, Rhode Island native Horatio S. Eustis came to Natchez to tutor Catherine Chotard. When they eventually married, they built this beautifully proportioned suburban villa. Modest in its detailing, *Oakland* features high ceilings, particularly fine woodwork, floor-length mahogany sash windows, and marble mantlepieces. Although a Greek Revival house, it has many of the qualities of the typical Southern plantation house. In 1857 Eustis sold *Oakland* to John Minor, Catherine's cousin, and his wife, Katherine Surget. Their descendants lived at *Oakland* until 1949.

THE BRIARS
1818, National Register of Historic Places

The Briars, named for the briar vines still growing in the woods, is located on a great bluff overlooking the Mississippi River and the Louisiana lowlands. Built in 1818 by John Perkins, *The Briars* was probably designed by noted architect Levi Weeks and is one of the finest planter's cottages in the area. It features a full-width front gallery recessed under a gabled roof, fanlighted doorways, and excellent Federal-style woodwork.

From 1828 to 1850 *The Briars* was rented to the family of William Burr Howell, son of the governor of New Jersey and cousin of Aaron Burr. In 1845 his daughter, Varina, called the "Rose of Mississippi," married West Point graduate Jefferson Davis, who was to become a hero of the Mexican War, a United States senator, secretary of war under President Franklin Pierce, and in 1861 the president of the Confederate States of America. *The Briars* was purchased in 1853 by Walter Irvine, whose family lived there until 1927.

The Briars has been completely restored and is run as a bed-and-breakfast by interior designers Robert E. Cannon and Newton Wilds.

LEFT: *Varina Howell married Jefferson Davis in 1845 in this front parlor.*

OPPOSITE: *The original rear gallery was enclosed and enlarged to create a forty-eight-foot drawing room with twin staircases and a screen of arches supported by fluted columns.*

HAWTHORNE
circa 1820-30, National Register of Historic Places

The precise origins of *Hawthorne* are uncertain. It was possibly built by real-estate investor Jonathan Thompson as early as 1818. Thompson and his family died of yellow fever in 1825 while they prepared to leave the city to stay at *Hawthorne*. The style of the house suggests to architectural historians that it was built in the late 1820s or early 1830s by the Overaker family. It was purchased in 1833 by Robert C. Dunbar, who died in the Civil War.

Hawthorne is a Federal-style house with a modest cottagelike exterior and generous interior spaces with beautifully detailed Federal-style mantlepieces and fanlighted doorways. The front gallery was probably an 1840s or 1850s remodeling. The dormers were added in the twentieth century.

RICHMOND *(OPPOSITE TOP)*
circa 1786, National Register of Historic Places

Richmond is a unique combination of three distinct architectural styles. The middle "English cottage" section was built around 1784-86 by Juan St. Germaine and is one of the oldest structures in Natchez. The front and rear galleries, once supported by round columns made of solid logs, were early additions. The west-facing front section, a splendid example of the Greek Revival style, was built by Levin R. Marshall in 1832. Generations of his family have been responsible for preserving this remarkable piece of American architectural heritage. The brick rear wing, almost Georgian in its severity, was added just prior to the Civil War. Among the Empire and Rococo Revival furnishings is the piano (opposite bottom) that was used to accompanied Jenny Lind, the "Swedish Nightingale," during her 1851 concert in Natchez.

When Jenny Lind visited Natchez in 1851, this piano was used to accompany her during a performance. It is one of two outstanding mid-nineteenth-century pianos at Richmond.

LONGWOOD
begun in 1860, National Historic Landmark

Longwood, the largest octagonal house in America, was the unfulfilled dream of planter and physician Haller Nutt. Designed by Philadelphia architect Samuel Sloan, *Longwood*—also called "Nutt's Folly"—was begun in the late 1850s with skilled craftsmen Sloan brought from Philadelphia. The design of the six-story, octagon-shaped house called for thirty-two rooms, each with its own balcony. It has a sixteen-sided cupola topped by a Byzantine dome.

When war was declared in 1861, workers abandoned the project to return home. Nutt moved his family into the finished basement, where the wine cellar, offices, and recreations rooms had been completed, to wait out the end of the war. Despite being a Union sympathizer, Nutt's rich cotton land was burned or confiscated by Union soldiers. Many of his museum-quality European furnishings and materials were seized by the Federal blockade. Nutt died of pneumonia in 1864. His wife, Julia, tried unsuccessfully to finish *Longwood.* Their descendants occupied the basement rooms for the next century. In 1970 the house was presented to the Pilgrimage Garden Club.

ABOVE: Abandoned tools still litter this unfinished room.
BELOW: The basement houses a dining room.

ELMS COURT
1836, National Register of Historic Places

Eliza and Catherine Evans, daughters of contractor Lewis Evans, purchased this land in 1836 and built the two-story center section of *Elms Court*. In 1852 it was sold to successful planter Francis Surget, who gave the estate as a wedding present to his daughter, Jane, and her husband, Ayres P. Merrill. The Merrills added the side wings and replaced the original portico with a two-story, ornamental cast-iron railed gallery. The Merrill's opposition to secession drove them north; Jane died without ever returning to *Elms Court*. President U. S. Grant appointed Ayres ambassador to Belgium in 1876.

James Surget of *Cherry Grove* took over *Elms Court* from his relatives and, in turn, made a present of it to his other daughter, Carlotta, and her husband, David McKittrick, whose descendants occupy *Elms Court* to this day.

Elms Court's resplendent gardens are of special interest to its present owner, Mrs. Grace McKittrick MacNeil, former president of the Girl Scouts of America. With the guidance and historically respectful planning of Jackson, Mississippi, landscape architect William Garbo, the gardens at *Elms Court* are among the finest private gardens in the country.

ABOVE, RIGHT, BELOW: The gardens at Elms Court seasonally feature camellias, azaleas, surprise lilies, tulips, and pansies.

OPPOSITE: Wisteria bloom on the back gallery of Elms Court.

GLOUCESTER
1803, National Register of Historic Places

This unusual mansion was begun in 1803 by Samuel Young and first named *Bellevue*. Winthrop Sargent, who came to Natchez in 1798 to be the first governor of the Mississippi Territory, purchased *Bellevue* and renamed it *Glouster Place* in honor of his Massachusetts birthplace. Sargent immediately doubled the size of the mansion, adding to the east side colossal two-story Tuscan columns and a second fanlighted entrance door. Though wealthy and powerful, Sargent was reportedly never a comfortable member of the Natchez social scene. In 1845 the younger of Sargent's two sons, George Washington Sargent, purchased *Gloucester*. He lived there a only short while until, at his own back door, a renegade Union soldier's bullet ended his life.

Unique in many ways, *Gloucester* combines the form of the one-room-deep planter's house, here terminated on each end by unusual half-octagons, with a monumental two-story portico. It features a brick-lined dry moat and a colonnaded gallery across the back.

GLENBURNIE
1833, National Register of Historic Places

Attorney Sturges Sprague and his wife, Frances, began *Glenburnie* in 1833 on land neighboring *Elms Court*. Their house is a typical one-story Mississippi planter's house with a full-width gallery recessed beneath a gabled roof. It features a fanlighted front door and turned columns similar to those at *The Briars*. This Federal-style house was built at about the same time that the Greek Revival style was introduced to Natchez.

In 1901 H. G. Bulkly built a Colonial Revival-inspired addition with galleries that was in harmony with the original design. *Glenburnie* received unwanted national attention as the site of the "Goat Castle Murder" of Jennie Merrill. Suspects included two neighbors living in squalor—literally, with goats and chickens—at nearby *Glenwood*.

THE SECOND CREEK

FAIR OAKS
circa 1822, National Register of Historic Places

Reliable records indicate *Fair Oaks*—originally called *Woodburne*—was built in the Second Creek neighborhood by mercantilist Henry W. Huntington in 1822. The entire house—floors, woodwork, roof—was constructed of virgin cypress. A typical planter's house, it is one room deep with a long, recessed gallery set beneath a gabled roof and supported by slender columns and open railings. The galleries are as well detailed as an interior room and in fact were used as living and dining rooms for many months of the year.

In 1856 the property was purchased by Dr. Orrick Metcalfe and his wife, who changed the name to *Fair Oaks*. Metcalfe was a country doctor who held both law and medical degrees. At times the servants' quarters functioned as a hospital. *Fair Oaks* is now the residence of Dr. Metcalfe's great-grandson, Bazile Lanneau, and his family.

OPPOSITE: This view from the dining room of Fair Oaks to the living room shows the repeated pattern of fanlighted doorways.

CHERRY GROVE
circa 1788, 1860s, National Register of Historic Places

Adventurer, seaman, and trader Pierre Surget lived aboard his own ship off the New Orleans coast for two years before settling in Natchez. He bartered his cargo of pig iron with the Natchez Indians for a large parcel of land in the Second Creek district of Natchez. Together with a twenty-five-hundred-acre land grant from the Spanish government, Surget built the first *Cherry Grove* in 1788. In the 1860s the house burned to the ground and was then immediately rebuilt. Today this extraordinarily lush piece of land is owned by the descendants of David McKittrick, who also own *Elms Court.*

ELGIN
circa 1780, 1840, National Register of Historic Places

Elgin was part of a Spanish land grant to Sir William Dunbar. The first house, a small one-story Federal style belonging to Sir William's brother, Archibald Dunbar, was thought to have been built around 1780. In 1840 *Elgin* was purchased by Dr. John Carmichael Jenkins, who married William Dunbar's granddaughter, Annis. Annis named the estate *Elgin* in honor of her grandfather's home in Scotland. Pennsylvania native Jenkins was a physician and planter but is best known for his innovative horticultural experiments. He produced hybrid species of orchids and fruit trees, studied soil depletion and new fertilization techniques, and developed methods of shipping fresh fruit packed in ice to northern markets.

Jenkins built an addition in 1840 that featured graceful two-story, double-tiered galleries. He extended it to the east in 1851 and to the west in 1855. The two-story brick kitchen with two-story tall columns was added in 1853. Tragically, both Dr. and Mrs. Jenkins died from the yellow-fever epidemic that devastated Natchez in 1855.

LANSDOWNE
1853, National Register of Historic Places

In 1853 wealthy planter "King" David Hunt gave a six-hundred-acre wedding present to his daughter, Charlotte, and her new husband, George Marshall, son of *Richmond*'s Levin Marshall. The couple built this Greek Revival mansion that, though modest on the outside, has some of the finest interior proportions and finishes in Natchez. *Lansdowne* is three rooms deep, features a center hall that extends the entire length of the house, and was the first residence to have its own gas-light plant.

Renegade Union soldiers attempted to loot *Lansdowne,* but Charlotte refused to give up her keys and was badly beaten and scarred. However, most of the family valuables, buried by a slave, were saved. *Lansdowne* was never remodeled, and the period furnishings and finishes have been carefully preserved. They include unusual interior marbling; hand-blocked Zuber wallpaper; Mallard, Signouret & Belter rosewood and mahogany furniture; Old Paris china; and Cornelius & Baker chandeliers.

The drawing room features original furniture and drapery and hand-blocked Zuber wallpaper.

ELGIN
circa 1780, 1840, National Register of Historic Places

Elgin was part of a Spanish land grant to Sir William Dunbar. The first house, a small one-story Federal style belonging to Sir William's brother, Archibald Dunbar, was thought to have been built around 1780. In 1840 *Elgin* was purchased by Dr. John Carmichael Jenkins, who married William Dunbar's granddaughter, Annis. Annis named the estate *Elgin* in honor of her grandfather's home in Scotland. Pennsylvania native Jenkins was a physician and planter but is best known for his innovative horticultural experiments. He produced hybrid species of orchids and fruit trees, studied soil depletion and new fertilization techniques, and developed methods of shipping fresh fruit packed in ice to northern markets.

Jenkins built an addition in 1840 that featured graceful two-story, double-tiered galleries. He extended it to the east in 1851 and to the west in 1855. The two-story brick kitchen with two-story tall columns was added in 1853. Tragically, both Dr. and Mrs. Jenkins died from the yellow-fever epidemic that devastated Natchez in 1855.

LANSDOWNE
1853, National Register of Historic Places

In 1853 wealthy planter "King" David Hunt gave a six-hundred-acre wedding present to his daughter, Charlotte, and her new husband, George Marshall, son of *Richmond*'s Levin Marshall. The couple built this Greek Revival mansion that, though modest on the outside, has some of the finest interior proportions and finishes in Natchez. *Lansdowne* is three rooms deep, features a center hall that extends the entire length of the house, and was the first residence to have its own gas-light plant.

Renegade Union soldiers attempted to loot *Lansdowne,* but Charlotte refused to give up her keys and was badly beaten and scarred. However, most of the family valuables, buried by a slave, were saved. *Lansdowne* was never remodeled, and the period furnishings and finishes have been carefully preserved. They include unusual interior marbling; hand-blocked Zuber wallpaper; Mallard, Signouret & Belter rosewood and mahogany furniture; Old Paris china; and Cornelius & Baker chandeliers.

The drawing room features original furniture and drapery and hand-blocked Zuber wallpaper.

MISTLETOE
1807, National Register of Historic Places

Mistletoe is the third house on the John Bisland's original land grant. Built in 1807 as a honeymoon cottage for his son, Peter Bisland, and Barbara Foster, *Mistletoe* is modest in size but elegantly detailed. It has a well-proportioned fan-lighted front door with two sidelights. The interior walls are finished in cypress with deeply molded Federal-style trim. The windowed gallery in the rear and two side wings were added in this century.

The sitting room features flush cypress boards and Federal-style molding.

THE NATCHEZ TRACE

BRANDON HALL
1856, National Register of Historic Places

Brandon Hall stands on land given in 1788 as a royal grant from Spanish King Carlos III to Frederick Calvit. In 1809 it was purchased by William Chew, who built a small house now incorporated as the "basement." In 1833 it was sold to Nathaniel Hoggatt, whose daughter, Charlotte, and her husband, Gerard Brandon III, ultimately built *Brandon Hall* in 1853. Gerard was the son of the first native-born governor of Mississippi. Brandon and Hoggatt family members lived at Brandon Hall until 1914, when it was sold to satisfy defaulted loans.

From 1914 to 1983 the property changed hands nine times. Large portions of the original grounds were sold off until only the house—seriously deteriorated— and forty acres remained intact. In 1983 it was purchased by Stanley Diefenthal, who began a remarkably thorough and respectful three-year restoration process that included the outbuildings and a complete relandscaping of the remaining grounds.

Brandon Hall stands again as one of the finest examples of Greek Revival architecture in Natchez, with more than three hundred feet of galleries supported by graceful classic columns. The new outbuildings, including a gazebo, harmonize with the historic architecture.

MOUNT LOCUST
circa 1780

After the American Revolution, the Trace was the most important land route between Nashville and the Old Southwest. As traffic increased, so did the demand for overnight rest stops. Eventually, more than fifty of these cabin-style inns dotted the pioneer road. *Mount Locust* was perhaps the oldest tavern on the south end of the Trace. It was built in 1780 by British rebel John Blommart and later operated by John Chamberlain.

The advent of the steamboat in the 1820s allowed two-way travel on the river, and the roadside inns slowly disappeared. Fortunately, *Mount Locust*, the last of these historic inns, is under the care of the National Park Service.

SPRINGFIELD
circa 1790

Andrew Jackson's early business ventures took him south from Nashville along the Old Trace where some friends, the Greens of *Springfield*, resided. On a return trip to Nashville, Jackson met a relative of the Greens, Rachel Donelson Robards, then married to the reportedly insanely jealous Lewis Robards. Fearful for her daughter's well-being, Rachel's mother asked Jackson to accompany Rachel back to the safety of her relatives in the Old Trace area of Natchez.

Fifteen joyous months later, in August of 1791, Andrew Jackson and Rachel Robards were married at *Springfield*. However, her divorce from Robards was never finalized by the Virginia Legislature—perhaps because of Robards's intervention—and this stigma hung over their lives forever.

HISTORIC JEFFERSON MILITARY COLLEGE
1811, National Register of Historic Places

Historic Jefferson Military College, was incorporated in 1802 by an act of the first General Assembly of the Mississippi Territory. The first educational institution in the Territory, it was named for President Thomas Jefferson. Forty-seven acres of land were donated by John and James Foster and Randal Gibson. Unfortunately, families in Natchez sent their children to Eastern schools and had little interest in the new college.

Finally, in 1811 *Jefferson College* opened as a preparatory school, and by 1817 it was a true college. Construction then began on the East Wing, designed by Natchez architect Levi Weeks. In 1830 the college purchased the Methodist Church, site of the 1817 Statehood Convention. The West Wing was completed in 1839. Before the Civil War, *Jefferson College* was at the forefront of intellectual and cultural development in frontier Mississippi and led the way in agricultural and scientific experimentation. Closed at the outbreak of the Civil War, it reopened in 1866 as a preparatory school and remained as such until it became *Jefferson Military College* at the beginning of the twentieth century. Regrettably, it closed its doors in 1964.

The Mississippi Department of Archives and History, with the aid of the nonprofit corporation The Friends of Jefferson College, undertook a complete restoration of the college. Visitors may now tour the college buildings and grounds as well as a nature trail that passes by Ellicott Springs.